CHAMP THORNTON

RADICALLY

DIFFERENT

#GOODBADNEW

A STUDENT'S GUIDE TO COMMUNITY

New Growth Press, Greensboro, NC 27404
www.newgrowthpress.com
Copyright © 2019 by Champ Thornton

All rights reserved. No part of this publication may be reproduced, stored
in a retrieval system, or transmitted in any form by any means, electronic,
mechanical, photocopy, recording, or otherwise, without the prior permission
of the publisher, except as provided by USA copyright law.

Unless otherwise indicated, Scripture quotations are taken from the ESV®
Bible (The Holy Bible, English Standard Version®). Copyright © 2001 by
Crossway, a publishing ministry of Good News Publishers. Used by permission.
All rights reserved.

Scripture quotations marked CSB are taken from the Christian Standard Bible.
Copyright © 2017 by Holman Bible Publishers. Used by permission. Christian
Standard Bible®, and CSB® are federally registered trademarks of Holman Bible
Publishers, all rights reserved.

Scripture quotations marked NIV are taken from the HOLY BIBLE, NEW
INTERNATIONAL VERSION®, NIV® Copyright © 1973, 1978, 1984, 2011 by Biblica,
Inc.® Used by permission. All rights reserved worldwide.

Scripture quotations marked NLT are taken from the *Holy Bible*, New Living
Translation, copyright © 1996, 2004, 2015 by Tyndale House Foundation. Used
by permission of Tyndale House Publishers, Inc., Carol Stream, Illinois 60188. All
rights reserved.

Cover Design: Faceout Books, faceoutstudio.com
Interior Design, illustration, and Typesetting: Scot McDonald

ISBN 978-1-948130-17-2 (Print)
ISBN 978-1-948130-18-9 (eBook)

Printed in the United States of America
26 25 24 23 22 21 20 19   1 2 3 4 5

Contents

Introduction

As you have been growing up, you have probably started to discover that life is getting complicated.

You've got to try to remember all your work for school and home. Then there are things you really enjoy, such as playing sports or video games and being with friends in person or online. You try to do several of these, and life starts to get busy. You think, *I can't keep up!* It becomes complex. *How do I handle this situation? What do I say now?* And it becomes difficult. *Why is that person making it so hard? What's the right thing to do in this relationship?*

It's tough to know what to do because almost nothing around us tells us how to live life God's way. We live in a broken world filled with people who don't love and obey God.

Yet God hasn't left us alone in this darkness. You may already believe the Bible is God's Word or at least believe that it's good for church topics. It talks about Jesus and going to heaven. But what about the tough stuff—especially people problems—that you face every day?

When you read it carefully, you'll find that the Bible shines light even on the dark and difficult parts of life. But don't take *my word* for it. Come see for yourself.

Learning how God's Word speaks to you and everything you're facing (and I mean *everything*) is one of the most important parts of growing up. It's not easy, but it's worth the effort. You'll have to use the mind God gave you to read and think. And you'll have to give of your time—that means you'll have to work at it because you won't always feel like it.

I've tried to provide some help to make your journey a bit easier. This book will direct you to specific parts of God's Word. And most weeks you'll read about a different type of relationship and discover for yourself what God says about it.

God is calling you to live in community with others—to live in the light of his Word. He wants you to be a bright light in a dark world.

Are you ready to be *radically different?*

How to Use This Book

The Big Story

The first four weeks of *Radically Different* prepare you for the remainder of the book. Week 1 begins with what is most important—God himself. Weeks 2–4 introduce the keys that unlock every door in life—the three lenses through which to look at every question. They are the following:

Week 2: Creation (*good*—God made everything "very good")
Week 3: Fall (*bad*—everything is messed up because of sin)
Week 4: Redemption (*new*—God sent Jesus to set things right)

In other words, when you're trying to figure something out, in relationships or anywhere else in life, ask these three questions:

- How is it good because God made it (Creation)?
- How is it messed up because of Adam and Eve's sin (the Fall)?
- And how has Jesus's death restored it to its original goodness—or even better (Redemption)?

CREATION	FALL	REDEMPTION
God made it . . .	We broke it . . .	Jesus fixes it.[1]
Good	Bad	New
God's World Designed	God's World Bent	God's World Restored

These three words—good, bad, new—are like three lenses of a telescope. You can, and should, look at everything in life through all three lenses.

The Weekly Plan

For the remainder of the weeks you'll use these three lenses to look at different topics. What's good/bad/new about your relationship with God? About your relationship with friends, parents, difficult people, etc.? (Hint: These lenses are for *any* area of life—like your own emotions, interests, plans, stuff, and activities.)

Since you're busy, this study requires your time only *three* days each week. And each day should not take you more than ten minutes to go through the introduction, pray, read the Bible verses listed, answer the questions, and reflect on what you've learned.

The Daily Fight

Each day you use this book, you'll likely face some struggles. First, your responsibilities or plans may easily crowd out your time in God's Word. So plan ahead. *Put your time with the Lord into your schedule.* Many people find it helpful to spend time with the Lord not long after waking up (see Mark 1:35).

Second, your heart may easily get distracted with other things to do. When it's time to be in God's Word, everything else may shout for your attention. Prepare for this. *Make your time in the Word a priority.* Nothing is more important than the Lord. Seek him and his priorities, and he'll take care of the other details in your life (Matthew 6:33).

Third, your focus may shift away from the Lord. Each week you'll look at a different topic related to relationships. Don't let your thinking about these things pull your attention from the main thing—God. *Keep your focus on the Lord himself.* This book isn't actually about what you think but about what you love. And we're to love God most of all (Mark 12:30).

Enough introductions—let's dive in!

WEEK ONE
GOD

This book is about relationships. But where to start? There are so many different people in your life—friends and family members, people at school and at church, fun people and not-so-fun people. Where do we dive in? Let's start where it's always best to begin—with God himself.

The Bible helps you see him, like a telescope helps you look at stars. When you look at a star—massive and erupting with energy—*without* a telescope, it seems like a tiny twinkle in the night sky. In the same way, some people imagine God as a distant and kind, bearded old man. Yet if you could really see what God is like, you'd be blown away! He's ablaze with limitless power, wisdom, beauty, and love. And this is how the Bible helps us see what God is truly like.

So when you open God's Word, remember to always look for who God is and what he's like. But before you start to read the passage of Scripture for each day this week, take time to pray from your heart this prayer or one like it.

PRAYER

"God, you have told us what you're like in your Word; please help me to really see what you've written, and most of all to see and get to know you better. In Jesus's name, Amen."

("Amen," means something like, "this is what I really mean," or "let it be so," or "I agree with what I've said." But most people usually just mean: "I'm done praying now.")

Day 1

Read John 1:14 and 18 (below). Remember, ask the Lord to help you understand what you've read.

{ 14 And the Word became flesh and dwelt among us, and we have seen his glory, glory as of the only Son from the Father, full of grace and truth. . . . 18 No one has ever seen God; the only God, who is at the Father's side, he has made him known. John 1:14, 18

▶ In John 1:14, someone is given the title "the Word." Whoever this is, he's communicating a very important message from God. Who do you think this is? (Hint: In the Bible who became human and lived among other human beings?)

▶ According to these verses, where can people see God? Who has made him known? Put verse 18 in your own words.

(When you see a lowercase letter after a verse number, that indicates a certain part of the verse. So, for example: verse "18a," refers to the first part of verse 18, usually up to the first punctuation mark, like a comma or semicolon. Verse 18b, would refer to the next section, and 18c would be the third section, etc.)

THINK ABOUT IT

If you want to see what God is like, look at Jesus. You can see what God is like in the powerful ways Jesus healed people, defeated demons, and controlled the weather. But as God's Son, Jesus revealed the Father in *everything* he did. Every kind word, every humble act of service, every moment of patience—all this shows you what our God is truly like in real-life ways we can understand.

Jesus revealed the Father in *everything* he did.

Day 2

Read 1 John 4:8 (below). (After you read, take time to pray the prayer at the beginning of this week, and then read 1 John 4:8 again.)

{ ⁸ Anyone who does not love does not know God, because God is love. 1 John 4:8

○ On Day 1, you learned how Jesus showed us exactly what God the Father is like. He revealed him. The question for today is what did Jesus reveal about the Father? What does 1 John 4:8 say that God is?

○ Which of the following does this verse NOT say? Cross through the wrong answers.

• God "does loving things."
• God "became love" by sending Jesus.
• God is "usually loving."
• God is love.

○ What do you think it means when John wrote, God is love?

○ Did you realize that God, at his very heart, *loves to love*? That's what he is actually like—at his core.

All this can be hard to think about. But here is the basic point: there has never, ever been a time when God was not full and overflowing with love. God *is* love. Take a moment and ask God to pour out his love into your heart today.

Day 3

So far this week, we've seen that Jesus shows us exactly what God is like, and what we learn about God is that he is full of love. That's just what he's like; no one twists his arm to be loving.

▶ But if God is love (not that he "became" love), what did God love *before* he created everything? Give this some thought, then write down your ideas.

Read John 17:24.

{ ²⁴ Father, I desire that they also, whom you have given me, may be with me where I am, to see my glory that you have given me because you loved me before the foundation of the world. John 17:24

▶ How does this verse answer the previous question? What was God doing before he made the universe? Whom was he loving?

This will not fit into our little human brains, but here's the mind-blowing truth: God has always been. And what he's always been is this: a loving Father to his Son. God the Father has always loved the Son, and the Son has always loved the Father (John 14:31). Together with the Holy Spirit, the Father and Son didn't make the world and people because they needed someone to love (they had each other, right?). Instead, because they were already so full of love—and always had been—the Father, Son, and Spirit created the world to share their love with others.

IN CLOSING

IT'S NOT ROCKET SCIENCE

If you've been around other Christians, you've probably heard the term "Trinity." This term is a compound word:

"tri" (three) + "[u]nity."

It refers to the fact that in the Bible there is one God in three persons: Father, Son, and Spirit. This seems impossible to figure out. But the Trinity is not an addition problem in math; it's not a formula in science.

Instead, the Tri-unity of God means that at his very core, God is *relational*. The Father has always loved the Son and Spirit. The Son and Spirit have always loved the Father and each other (John 14:31; 16:14–15; 17:24). It's in God's deepest nature to love and show love to others (Hosea 11:9). And he's always been that way. C. S. Lewis, author of the Chronicles of Narnia said it this way:

❝In Christianity God is not a static thing—not even a person—but a dynamic, pulsating activity, a life, almost a kind of drama. Almost, if you will not think me irreverent, a kind of dance. . . . [The] pattern of this three-Personal life is . . . a great fountain of energy and beauty spurting up at the very centre of reality.❞ 2

So, for Christians, when God says he loves you, he means it from the bottom of his heart. When you ask him to show compassion or mercy, you don't have to convince him or try to make him do something he doesn't want to do. The Tri-unity of God means that he is—and always has been—full and overflowing with love.

WEEK TWO
GOOD

GREAT TO MEET YOU DUDE...

CHALLENGE

Open your Bible to Genesis 1 and count how many times God said what he made was good.

The Bible begins with the story of how God made the world. Again and again, he sized up what he'd made, and he said it was "good."

All of it was "very good" (Genesis 1:31)! The whole created universe was top quality. No defects, no flaws, nothing to displease or disappoint.

What made it all so fantastic? The answer is that everything, like a mirror, reflected what God himself is like (Psalm 19:1). God made the universe for the loving reason of showing people how amazing he is, how beautiful, and how kind!

What's your favorite song? Whatever it is, could you imagine getting to meet the artist who wrote it or sings it? Forever after, whenever you heard the song, you would always think of the artist.

This is *why* God created. He made everything good to remind us of him! But here's a new question to think about this week: If we're part of God's very good creation, *how* does he want us to live? (Before you answer, take a moment to talk to the Lord.)

PRAYER

"Father, you are the creator and sustainer of the universe. Thank you for making everything and for making it all so good. Help me give thanks to you through the day for all the things I enjoy. They all come from your good heart. And as I enjoy the creation, help me to enjoy you even more. In Jesus's name, Amen."

Day 1

This week we're looking at the *goodness* of creation. Read the first part of Genesis 1:26.

> Then God said, "Let us make man in our image, after our likeness." Genesis 1:26a

▶ According to what design did God craft man and woman?

THINK ABOUT IT

Made in God's image, every person has dignity and value. All creation reflects its Creator in some way. But humans were designed to resemble God in a special way. The portrait of a president hanging in a government building looks like the president, but it also represents the president's authority in that location. In the same way, God has put his representatives all over the earth. Men and women were created to represent and resemble their Creator.

Now read the second part of Genesis 1:26.

[God said:] "And let [the man and the woman] have dominion over the fish of the sea and over the birds of the heavens and over the livestock and over all the earth and over every creeping thing that creeps on the earth." Genesis 1:26b

▶ As God's representatives, what are humans supposed to do on earth?

▶ Read Genesis 2:15 (below). Circle the words that show other ways that humans represent God through their actions.

The LORD God took the man and put him in the garden of Eden to work it and keep it. Genesis 2:15

Being made "in the image of God" teaches that we, like him, should **creatively cultivate** the world around us. List three areas that you can protect and develop, as you're encouraged to do in Genesis 1:26b and 2:15. Following are several items listed to get you started:

▶ I can cultivate my part of God's good world by

✱ making my room more orderly and attractive.
✱ helping with dishes and laundry.
✱ organizing my homework (or helping someone who might be struggling in this area).

Day 2

God made everything good. Read Genesis 2:16–17 (below). In these verses, what is the first command God gave?

> ¹⁶ And the Lᴏʀᴅ God commanded the man, saying, "You may surely eat of every tree of the garden, ¹⁷ but of the tree of the knowledge of good and evil you shall not eat, for in the day that you eat of it you shall surely die." Genesis 2:16–17

● According to 1 Timothy 6:17 (below), why did God give us everything he's created?

● Everything God made is good and to be enjoyed. If God wants you to enjoy what he's created, how does that change your thoughts about what God is like?

> As for the rich in this present age, charge them not to be haughty, nor to set their hopes on the uncertainty of riches, but on God, who richly provides us with everything to enjoy. 1 Timothy 6:17

Day 3

▶ Everything God created is good. Reread Genesis 2:16–17. In your own words, what does God command in verse 17?

▶ If everything God had created was good, why do you think God even gave rules to be obeyed?

Part of the goodness of creation is that God designed it to be enjoyed and cultivated *within boundaries*. In creation, as in board games, there are "rules of play" that make life fun and good. Many of these rules of play are commanded by God in the Bible. They tell us how life works best. For examples of these very good rules which relate to relationships, read Exodus 20:12–17.

> "¹² Honor your father and your mother, that your days may be long in the land that the LORD your God is giving you. ¹³ You shall not murder. ¹⁴ You shall not commit adultery. ¹⁵ You shall not steal. ¹⁶ You shall not bear false witness against your neighbor. ¹⁷ You shall not covet your neighbor's house; you shall not covet your neighbor's wife, or his male servant, or his female servant, or his ox, or his donkey, or anything that is your neighbor's." Exodus 20:12–17

THINK ABOUT IT

Did you know that these rules of play aren't just written in words? God's rules are hardwired into creation itself. God created an order or structure in life that you can't escape. For example, isn't lying or murdering considered wrong by most people in most cultures? Selfless friendships are appreciated by almost everyone, right? And don't you agree that people need to love and be loved by others? God designed his world, even though it's broken by sin, to operate according to his rules of play.

● Read Deuteronomy 10:13 (below). And then rephrase it in your own words.

{ "[God requires you] to keep the commandments and statutes of the LORD, which I am commanding you today for your good."
Deuteronomy 10:13

● Are there any of God's rules of play that you find difficult to keep? Pause to talk to the Lord about your struggle.

IN CLOSING

a REAL PaNE

Did you know that you can look at everything in this world just like you look at a window? You can look at something or you can look *through* something.

At least this is what a pastor named George Herbert thought. Born in Wales (which borders England) in 1593, he only lived 39 years. But what a full life!

As a young man, he first served in the royal court of the British king, James I. He wrote speeches for the king. After a few years, George believed God was calling him to be a pastor. Now he would speak for another King. God had given him a talent with words. At heart, George was a poet.

Whatever God was teaching him, George tried to express it by writing poetry. George Herbert knew that God had created every-thing. So to George, enjoying what God had made without seeing the God who made it was like looking *at* a window, but not looking *through* it. George said it like this:

Teach me, my God and King,
In all things Thee to see,
And what I do in anything,
To do it as for Thee.

A man who looks on glass,
On it may fix his sight,
Or, if he pleases, through it pass,
To view the heavens bright.[3]

In other words, you can look at your abilities in sports, or you can look *through* them. You can look at your dinner, or look through it. At your tech devices, or through them. At your relationships, or through them.

What lies beyond everything that you enjoy? God himself. The Creator. He made everything for your enjoyment and for his praise. So don't just look at life. Look *through* it, see the Creator, and give him thanks.

WEEK THREE
BAD

Remember how Genesis 1 and 2 explain that God created the world good? Well, in the very next chapter of Genesis, the story jumps from good to bad.

This "badness" doesn't mean destroyed, like when a big car wreck means your vehicle is totaled and headed for the junkyard. Instead, it means that everything God made has been twisted and corrupted—bent out of its original shape.

Nothing on earth escapes this damage. Mankind's relationship with God is broken. Our relationships with other people are broken. Our relationship with this world is broken. And our relationship to our own self is broken. Every single good thing, all that God had made, is warped—bent—by this badness.

Did You Know?

Bible teachers call the cause of this badness the "fall" because it's the story of how the first humans (Adam and Eve) fell from their original goodness. At the start they had been good and righteous and holy, but then came the fall.

What happened? That's what we'll look at this week. Here's a prayer to get you started:

PRAYER

"Lord, you are the giver of all good rules. How kind of you to tell us how life is best lived. Please forgive me for living as my own boss, making and obeying my own laws. Help me really believe that your ways are good and best. In Jesus's name. Amen."

Day 1

The badness begins. Read Genesis 3:1.

> Now the serpent was more crafty than any other beast of the field that the LORD God had made. He said to the woman, "Did God actually say, 'You shall not eat of any tree in the garden'?" Genesis 3:1

○ In this verse Satan, who was disguised as a snake, asks Eve a question. Write down his question word-for-word as it appears in your Bible.

○ Compare Genesis 3:1 with Genesis 2:16–17 (see Week 2, Day 2). What had God *actually* said? Explain how Satan twisted God's actual statement.

○ Circle the aspect of God's character that Satan was attacking:

Justice

Forgiveness

Holiness

Majesty

Goodness

▶ In your own words, describe how Satan wanted God to appear in the minds of Adam and Eve.

▶ List five things you really, really want badly. (To get you started, this could be a friendship. Or is it a skill? An app or game?) Think and pray about how you might be missing the goodness of what you *already have* been given by God. (Hint: These blessings might include family, forgiveness, second chances, love, acceptance, etc.)

Day 2

Let's continue to look at the bad that has bent God's good world. Read Genesis 3:4–6.

> ⁴ But the serpent said to the woman, "You will not surely die. ⁵ For God knows that when you eat of it your eyes will be opened, and you will be like God, knowing good and evil." ⁶ So when the woman saw that the tree was good for food, and that it was a delight to the eyes, and that the tree was to be desired to make one wise, she took of its fruit and ate, and she also gave some to her husband who was with her, and he ate.
> Genesis 3:4–6

● From these verses, use your own words to describe what three things attracted Eve to the fruit that God had forbidden.

● At the moment of her temptation, what did Eve value most? What did she no longer value?

By eating the very appealing fruit, Eve chose to worship something instead of God. This kind of God-substitute is what the Bible calls an "idol." *Idolatry* is when you treat something God made (something good) as too important (more important than God).

THINK ABOUT IT

A stone is a thing created by God, but when it's carved into a statue and people pray to it like a god, it becomes an idol. It's something that's created that's being treated like it's the Creator. And to this day, sin—at its heart—is loving something God has given more than loving the God who gave it.

Here's an example: When you love something like sports or friendship so much that you're willing to lie just a little bit in order to make everything work out the way you want, what is going on? You are loving the good thing (sports, friendship) more than God, who commands us to tell the truth.

▶ Is there anything that you love too much? Think about things you like to do. Or things you own—or *want* to own. Pick one thing which you're starting to realize that you love too much. In your own words, describe how you can tell that it's too important to you.

Day 3

Today our study of badness continues. Read Genesis 3:7–13 (below). Circle everything in this passage that was affected by Adam and Eve's sin.

7 Then the eyes of both were opened, and they knew that they were naked. And they sewed fig leaves together and made themselves loincloths. 8 And they heard the sound of the LORD God walking in the garden in the cool of the day, and the man and his wife hid themselves from the presence of the LORD God among the trees of the garden. 9 But the LORD God called to the man and said to him, "Where are you?" 10 And he said, "I heard the sound of you in the garden, and I was afraid, because I was naked, and I hid myself." 11 He said, "Who told you that you were naked? Have you eaten of the tree of which I commanded you not to eat?" 12 The man said, "The woman whom you gave to be with me, she gave me fruit of the tree, and I ate." 13 Then the LORD God said to the woman, "What is this that you have done?" The woman said, "The serpent deceived me, and I ate."
Genesis 3:7–13

▶ **Your relationship with yourself.** How did sin affect what Adam and Eve thought about themselves? How did they feel inside after sinning? What does Genesis 3:7–13 say about this?

▶ **Your relationship with other people.** How did sin affect Adam and Eve's relationship with each other? How should they have treated each other instead?

▶ **Your relationship to the space around you.** Read Genesis 3:16–19. How did sin affect Adam and Eve's responsibility to protect, cultivate, and develop their world?

> ¹⁶ To the woman he said, "I will surely multiply your pain in child-bearing; in pain you shall bring forth children. Your desire shall be contrary to your husband, but he shall rule over you." ¹⁷ And to Adam he said, "Because you have listened to the voice of your wife and have eaten of the tree of which I commanded you, 'You shall not eat of it,' cursed is the ground because of you; in pain you shall eat of it all the days of your life; ¹⁸ thorns and thistles it shall bring forth for you; and you shall eat the plants of the field. ¹⁹ By the sweat of your face you shall eat bread, till you return to the ground, for out of it you were taken; for you are dust, and to dust you shall return." Genesis 3:16–19

▶ **Your relationship with God.** Read Genesis 3:22–24. How did sin affect Adam and Eve's walk with the Lord?

> ²² Then the Lᴏʀᴅ God said, "Behold, the man has become like one of us in knowing good and evil. Now, lest he reach out his hand and take also of the tree of life and eat, and live forever—" ²³ therefore the Lᴏʀᴅ God sent him out from the garden of Eden to work the ground from which he was taken. ²⁴ He drove out the man, and at the east of the garden of Eden he placed the cherubim and a flaming sword that turned every way to guard the way to the tree of life. Genesis 3:22–24

▶ What do you think? If it is true that sin affects everything, then what's wrong with the common piece of advice to "follow your heart"?

DON'T MOVE THE GOALPOSTS

On New Year's Day 1965, the Michigan Wolverine football team defeated the Oregon State Beavers, 34 to 7. As the whistle blew, ending the Rose Bowl game, hundreds of cheering Michigan fans stormed the field. In a victory celebration they began pulling down the opponent's goalposts.

This is no small task! In American football, goalposts are thirty feet tall, with the bottom crosspiece ten feet off the ground. They also usually weigh about five hundred pounds and can withstand 115-mile-per-hour winds. But if you get a dozen people to sit or pull on them, down they come. And often people get hurt.

A bent goalpost is a great picture of how the good of Creation and the bad of the Fall fit together. Everything in the created universe has a good and intended structure (just as goalposts are meant to stand straight up). But since the Fall, people exert force to bend God's structures in their own directions, away from God's original design.[4]

Sin isn't some negative force that exists apart from creation. Instead, sin takes God's good creation and bends it. For example, lying (a bad thing) is still communication (a good thing). A criminal (a bad thing) is still a human made in God's image (a good thing). And a glutton (a bad thing) binges on food (a good thing).

As Christians, we should

1. try to understand what is good in everything.

2. reject the ways people have bent anything away from what God intended.

3. work to re-bend what has been bent by sin, bringing it closer to what God intended.

WEEK FOUR

NEW

COMING SOON

NEW CREATION

et's review. When sin entered the world, it broke the good relationships that had once existed between humans and God, between humans and nature, and among humans themselves. Like adding poison to a pot of soup, everything good was tainted with bad.

But God had a plan to set everything *right*.

Not to throw everything out . . . and make *all new things*,

but to fix what was broken . . . to make *all things new.*[5]

And this is our topic for the week. To make everything new, God would send his own Son, Jesus, to heal broken relationships (Colossians 1:20). Through Christ, God would reconcile everything to himself. Things that are part good and part bad would be made new and better (Revelation 21:5).

Do you like movies? Reading about Jesus's life in the Gospels (Matthew, Mark, Luke, and John) is like watching trailers previewing the great "new-creation movie" to come. Jesus brings healing, happiness, and life. And he removes sickness, suffering, and death. As we think about the newness that Jesus brings, here's a prayer for the week.

PRAYER

"Father, thank you for sending Jesus to fix this messy world and my messy life. I see good things in my life (my relationships, my decisions, my skills, my personality, my body), but I see bad things as well. Please take this good-bad combo and make it *new*. Make me more like Jesus in all areas of my life. In Jesus's name. Amen."

Day 1

What does it mean to be "new"? Read Matthew 5:13–16.

> 13 [Jesus said,] "You are the salt of the earth, but if salt has lost its taste, how shall its saltiness be restored? It is no longer good for anything except to be thrown out and trampled under people's feet. 14 You are the light of the world. A city set on a hill cannot be hidden. 15 Nor do people light a lamp and put it under a basket, but on a stand, and it gives light to all in the house. 16 In the same way, let your light shine before others, so that they may see your good works and give glory to your Father who is in heaven." Matthew 5:13–16

● What does Jesus mean when he says that Christians are to be "salt" and "light" in this world?

DID YOU KNOW?

In the ancient world, with no electricity or refrigerators, people packed meat in salt to prevent decay. And when the sun went down, without electric lights, it was really dark.

iStock.com/Olga_Mallari

▶ What does Jesus say in Matthew 5:15 is the wrong thing to do with light?

▶ Can you think of one area of decay or darkness in which you can be salt and light today? Pray about it and ask the Lord to bring one area to mind. Write down your thoughts.

▶ As a Christian, how might you be tempted to respond (unbiblically) to the bad of darkness and decay that exists in God's good world?

Day 2

God is making all things *new*. That's our topic. Read 2 Corinthians 5:17 slowly, several times.

> Therefore, if anyone is in Christ, he is a new creation. The old has passed away; behold, the new has come.
> 2 Corinthians 5:17

○ Write down the words of the verse to answer this question: What does this verse say is true for everyone who is a Christian (everyone who is "in Christ")?

○ What do you think it means to be a "new creation"?

THINK ABOUT IT

As a Christian, you live in two worlds. On your birthday, years ago, you were born into this world, a world which contains a mix of "good" and "bad." If you're a Christian, you've also been "born *again*" and belong to the world to come—the "new" creation. Since you are a citizen of the new creation, God wants you to live your life in a way that fits the *new* creation.

Read Ephesians 4:22–24 (below). You may also want to look up and read verses 25–32.

> 22 [God wants you] to put off your old self, which belongs to your former manner of life and is corrupt through deceitful desires, 23 and to be renewed in the spirit of your minds, 24 and to put on the new self, created after the likeness of God in true righteousness and holiness.
> Ephesians 4:22–24

● List at least two "old creation" actions or attitudes you should "put off" and at least two "new creation" actions or attitudes you should "put on." Ask the Lord to help you with this today.

Day 3

God has made us part of his new creation. So he also wants us to live in a way that fits our newness. Read Titus 2:9–10.

{ ⁹ Teach slaves [servants or employees] to be subject to their masters [employers] in everything, to try to please them, not to talk back to them, ¹⁰ and not to steal from them, but to show that they can be fully trusted, so that in every way they will make the teaching about God our Savior attractive. Titus 2:9–10 NIV

○ Circle the "put off" actions that these verses say that servants or employees should not do.

○ Write down the "put on" actions that these verses say that servants or employees should do.

○ Re-read verse 10 (above). As Christians live new-creation lives, what is the *reason* in this verse for doing or not doing certain things? Put the last part of this verse in your own words.

DID YOU KNOW? ----

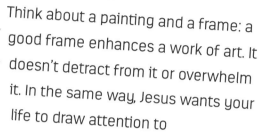

If God's new creation is like a beautiful painting, your life is like the frame.

Think about a painting and a frame: a good frame enhances a work of art. It doesn't detract from it or overwhelm it. In the same way, Jesus wants your life to draw attention to the amazingly wonderful new creation he will finish one day. (And you are part of that new creation too!)

▶ When people look at you, what do they see? Do they see more "old creation" or "new creation"? Ask the Lord to use you to draw attention to the beauty of his new creation.

a Pillar of the Faith

Here is a true story: There once lived a man named Simeon (AD 390–459). He loved God, but he didn't like the world he lived in. About seventy years before he was born it became cool to be known as a Christian. Instead of the Roman Empire trying to kill Christians (throwing them to the lions, etc.), now Christianity was the official religion of the empire. So lots of people—even people who didn't really believe in Jesus—wanted to say they were Christians.

So in Simeon's day it was hard to tell who was a real Christian and who was faking it. The "good" and the "bad" were all mixed together, like a block of marble with swirls of different colors throughout.

Then Simeon had an idea. He wanted to try to separate the good from the bad. He wanted to worship God apart from the world. So he decided to make a pillar and live on a small platform at the top of it, far out of reach of the bad world below. He wanted to live for God "upstairs," high above the everyday world "downstairs." Simeon's first pillar was nine feet tall, but that wasn't far enough. So he had another one built, this time around fifty feet off the ground. Food was sent up using a rope and pulley. He lived there for thirty-seven years!

But there was a problem with this arrangement. (Actually there were lots of problems, and bathing was not the least of them!) For starters, Simeon couldn't escape the effects of the Fall because Simeon (a sinner) took *himself* with him to the top of the pillar! But there was another issue: Jesus has redeemed his people so they can live right in the middle of this good but fallen world—to be salt and light among decay and darkness. People are not meant to live away from others in the world.

Don't be like Simeon. Christianity isn't for "upstairs" living—just for Sundays or in your daily Bible time. Christianity is an "upstairs *and downstairs*" way of life that's meant to be lived out 24-7 with other Christians in front of the world.

WEEK FIVE
LISTENING TO GOD

Heads Up!
You can sum up the last three weeks on Creation, Fall, and Redemption with the words *good*, *bad*, and *new*. Each future week in *Radically Different* will study a topic using these three words.

Within every week
- **Day 1** will look at that week's topic through the lens of how God made it "good."
- **Day 2** will focus on how it has been twisted by the fall ("bad").
- **Day 3** will explore how Jesus is making it "new."

What comes to mind when you think about these actions?
- Swinging a mighty hammer
- Shooting beams of fiery energy
- Wielding a razor-sharp blade
- Controlling the effects of water

These are actions of a pretty amazing team of superheroes, right? Aquaman, Thor, Ironman, and Wolverine may come to mind. (Please accept my apology for including heroes from both Marvel Comics and DC Comics in the same sentence!) But each of these actions is an image the Bible uses to describe itself.

The Bible is powerful. It's like a hammer (Jeremiah 23:29), water (Ephesians 5:26), sword (Hebrews 4:12), and fire (Jeremiah 23:29). When you open your Bible and read, it may seem like you're in control, like you're the one doing something. After all, you're the one doing the reading.

But when you read God's Word, did you know that something is being done *to you*? God is at work. He is using his Word to change you and help you.

PRAYER

"Lord, thank you for giving us your Word to speak to us. How awful life would be—how in the dark we would be—if you had been silent. Help me learn about your Word this week and to be a better listener to you. In Jesus's name I pray these things. Amen."

Day 1 (GOOD)

No surprise, but there are a lot of *good* things to say about the Bible. We've already seen that it's like a hammer, sword, fire, and water. But that's just the beginning.

Read Deuteronomy 8:3.

> And he humbled you and let you hunger and fed you with manna, which you did not know, nor did your fathers know, that he might make you know that man does not live by bread alone, but man lives by every word that comes from the mouth of the LORD.
> Deuteronomy 8:3

⯈ If you were explaining this verse to a first grader, what would you say?

⯈ God made human beings to survive not just on physical food (bread, meat, mac and cheese, etc.) but on something else. What?

⯈ Why do you think God says his Word, the Bible, is like bread (food)? Circle all that apply. Which of the following does God's Word, our spiritual food, do for you?

✱ Makes you stronger

✱ Improves math scores

✱ Provides endurance

✱ Gives health

✱ Reduces body fat

God made his Word to help you. If you've not been regularly in his Word, ask the Lord to help you "eat" more often, more regularly. A healthy feast awaits you each day.

Day 2 (BAD)

Read Genesis 3:8-9.

> 8 And they heard the sound of the LORD God walking in the garden in the cool of the day, and the man and his wife hid themselves from the presence of the LORD God among the trees of the garden. 9 But the LORD God called to the man and said to him, "Where are you?" Genesis 3:8-9

◉ We've already discussed how Adam and Eve made a choice to disobey God. But *after* Adam and Eve sinned, what did they do when they heard the Lord?

Have you ever turned on the light and seen a bug scurry out of sight? Ever since sin entered the world (and our hearts), we've all run away from God and his Word just like the bug. Everyone is born in darkness (Romans 1:21; Ephesians 4:18) and tends to avoid the light. In fact, the Bible says that it's like all of us are born with a serious spiritual disability. We don't see clearly.

◉ Write out Psalm 119:18 (below) in your own words. Make this your own prayer.

> Open my eyes, that I may behold wondrous things out of your law. Psalm 119:18

Throughout this week, pray this short verse as a prayer to God from your heart.

Day 3 (NEW)

In the gospels Jesus healed many blind people. At the beginning of that day, they were in darkness, but after meeting Jesus, they could see! Did you know that Jesus also healed *spiritual* blindness? Read Luke 24:45.

> Then he opened their minds to understand the Scriptures.
> Luke 24:45

▶ With new spiritual sight what could these men now see?

Did you know that Jesus still heals like this today? Jesus takes away the blindness and darkness that you learned about yesterday. He is the one who gives spiritual sight and light. If you want to understand the Bible, you must first trust Jesus. He came to make all things *new*. This includes the way you read the Bible, the way you view its truths, and the way you think about God. Read Acts 26:17b–18a.

> [17] [The Lord said to Paul] "I am sending you [18] to open their eyes, so that they may turn from darkness to light and from the power of Satan to God, that they may receive forgiveness of sins." Acts 26:17b–18a

▶ Do you know a friend or family member who doesn't believe the Bible? Pray Acts 26:17b–18a for them. Pray that God gives you an opportunity to talk with them about what Jesus means to you.

OPEN YOUR EYES

It can be frustrating to be around people who never stop talking about themselves. *Me, me, me!*

And then there are the people who "*humble* brag" on social media.

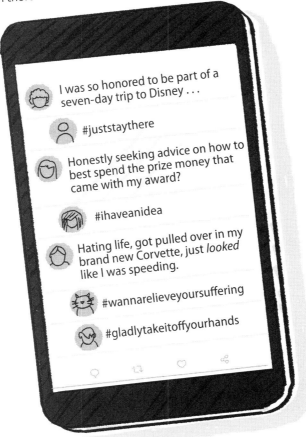

> I was so honored to be part of a seven-day trip to Disney . . .
>
> #juststaythere
>
> Honestly seeking advice on how to best spend the prize money that came with my award?
>
> #ihaveanidea
>
> Hating life, got pulled over in my brand new Corvette, just *looked* like I was speeding.
>
> #wannarelieveyoursuffering
>
> #gladlytakeitoffyourhands

The Bible is spectacular because even though it tells us about some amazing people, it doesn't brag. In fact, that's one reason you can know it's real and true.

Imagine a different scenario. What if *you* had been responsible to tell the story about Jesus's disciples (the men who would become the biggest leaders in the early church)? What would you have said about them? Would you have told about how quickly they learned from Jesus? How they showed amazing potential?

But the four Gospels (Matthew, Mark, Luke, and John) seem to go out of their way to show how messed up the disciples were. Especially when you read the gospel according to Mark, you can see that these disciples repeatedly just didn't get it (Mark 4:13; 7:17; 8:14–16). Jesus had to rebuke them (4:12–13), and eventually they abandoned Jesus for a while (14:50).

Imagine. If the gospel writers were just making up all this stuff about Jesus, why would they tell honest and some-times ugly stories about church leaders? The honesty of the Gospels shows that they weren't telling lies. Instead, they were spreading the truth about what happened, even when it showed that Jesus's followers could be weak and "blind." But the good news is that Jesus could heal their blindness then and he can heal *your* blindness today.

Keep praying for clearer spiritual sight, and keep reading his trustworthy Word. The Lord will open your eyes to see the truth. You can depend on it.

WEEK SIX
TALKING TO GOD

I like detective stories, especially the ones about Sherlock Holmes. Holmes, a genius who sees important details that other people miss, uses his powers of observation to solve mysteries or capture criminals. Some stories tell how Sherlock finds a way to enter a locked or hidden room (such as in "The Red-Headed League"). And often the stories end with the detective luring someone out of hiding in order to talk with this person who had been so hard to track down (such as in the story "A Study in Scarlet").

Sometimes it's easy to think that prayer is like solving a puzzling mystery. With this mind-set, you have to work really hard to unlock a secret entrance to God. Or you have to go through careful steps in order to capture his attention and talk to him. But prayer doesn't require a hidden access code or password. And you don't have to be a spiritual genius to engage the Lord in conversation. Basically, prayer is talking with the God who wants to hear you.

PRAYER

"Thank you that in your Word, you not only talk to me, but you also help me know how to talk to you. Lord, will you please teach me to pray? Help me grow in this area of life. In Jesus's name. Amen."

Day 1 (GOOD)

Before sin entered the world, what did God think about prayer? Read Genesis 3:8.

> And they heard the sound of the LORD God walking in the garden in the cool of the day, and the man and his wife hid themselves from the presence of the LORD God among the trees of the garden. Genesis 3:8

● What was the Lord doing?

Apparently, God had done this before. Adam and Eve recognized who was walking in the garden. They had talked with God previously. This shouldn't be a surprise when you see what Jesus said in Matthew 7:11.

> If you then, who are evil, know how to give good gifts to your children, how much more will your Father who is in heaven give good things to those who ask him! Matthew 7:11

● According to this verse, how would you describe the Father's heart toward the prayers of his children?

● Take a moment to just tell your Father what is on your heart and mind—what's bothering you, worrying you, distracting you, or making you happy.

Day 2 (BAD)

NO SERVICE

Doesn't bad cell phone or Wi-Fi coverage drive you crazy? Did you know that sin does the same kind of thing to prayer? Read Psalm 66:18.

> If I had cherished iniquity in my heart, the Lord would not have listened. Psalm 66:18

▶ Rephrase this verse using your own words.

▶ According to this verse, what is most true? (Circle one.) If I _____ sin, the Lord will not hear me.

commit   stumble into   love   struggle with

Did you know that one kind of prayer always gets through? Read Proverbs 28:13.

> Whoever conceals his transgressions will not prosper, but he who confesses and forsakes them will obtain mercy. Proverbs 28:13

▶ What clears away this sin-barrier to prayer? What kind of prayer does God always love to hear?

▶ Are there sins that you don't want to stop doing? Do you find yourself, when you think about it, actually wanting to keep doing what *you* want to do, instead of what God wants? If so, will you confess those sins to the Lord? (See page 53 for some ideas of how this kind of confession might sound. Use the Bible's words to form your own prayer to the Lord.)

Day 3 (NEW)

Jesus opened the pathway to God. Read John 14:13.

> [Jesus said,] "Whatever you ask in my name, this I will do, that the Father may be glorified in the Son." John 14:13

○ This verse describes a certain way to pray. According to this verse, how should you pray? Fill in the blank.

Christians pray _____ Jesus's _____.

○ So in your own words, what does it mean when you pray "in Jesus's name"?

○ Does praying in Jesus's name mean you can ask for anything you could ever possibly want? What kinds of prayers do you think *fit* "Jesus's name"? Write down two things that you can ask God for "in Jesus's name."

DID YOU KNOW?

When you do something in the name of someone else, you are acting as if you were in that person's shoes. (Like when someone making a citizen's arrest says, "I arrest you in the name of the law," he or she is standing in the place of the police.) Acting "in the name of" someone else means doing something as if you were the other person—using their resources, abilities, authority, and privileges.

IN THE NAME OF THE LAW...

KEEP IT FRESH

In church you might have heard some people say a lot of the same things when they pray. For example,

- "Dear heavenly Father"
- "In Jesus's name, Amen"
- "Lead, guide, and direct us"
- "We just want to thank you . . ."
- "Thank you for this day."
- "Bless the gift and the giver"

Perhaps you can think of other phrases that may have lost their meaning because they've been used so often.

But when it comes to prayer, the Bible is packed with variety. When you pray, there are even different ways to position your *body*. People pray while

- spreading arms wide (Exodus 9:29).
- lifting hands (1 Timothy 2:8).
- kneeling down (Daniel 6:10).
- bowing down on the ground (Exodus 34:8).
- lying down (Ezra 10:1).
- standing up (Genesis 24:13).
- sitting (2 Samuel 7:18).
- looking up (John 17:1).
- looking down (Luke 18:13).

And there are different ways to arrange your *words*. On the next page is a small sample of different prayers for different circumstances. However you may feel at a particular time, the Lord has provided prayers for you. He invites you to share your heart with him (Psalm 62:8).

Prayers Confessing Sin

"Have mercy on me, O God, according to your steadfast love; according to your abundant mercy blot out my transgressions. Wash me thoroughly from my iniquity, and cleanse me from my sin!" (Psalm 51:1–2; see also Psalm 40:11–12.)

Prayers Praising God

"Worthy are you, our Lord and God, to receive glory and honor and power, for you created all things, and by your will they existed and were created." (Revelation 4:11; see also 1 Chronicles 29:10–13.)

Prayers Making Requests

"And it is my prayer that your love may abound more and more, with knowledge and all discernment, so that you may approve what is excellent, and so be pure and blameless for the day of Christ, filled with the fruit of righteousness that comes through Jesus Christ, to the glory and praise of God." (Philippians 1:9–11; see also 2 Thessalonians 2:16–17.)

WEEK SEVEN
WORSHIPING GOD

"Everyone worships, even people who don't believe in God."

Do you agree with this statement? Is it really true? Take a moment to think it over.

The real question isn't whether everyone worships. The issue is *what* do people worship?

In other words, all people have something they love and value the most. Every person relies on something to make life work—to provide happiness or peace or whatever is desired. Everyone has a "god" who provides what he or she "needs."

For example, some people treasure *relationships*; they hope that friends will make them happy. Other people value what *achievement* can give: success, money, fame. Whatever you're hoping will give you what you most deeply want, that's what you worship, even if you don't literally kneel before it or sing songs to it.

So it's true that we all worship something.

PRAYER

"Lord, you are the true God, the only God. You made everything good, but not *best*. You are the best. Please help me believe this and live like this. Give me grace to see how amazing you are and to treasure you above everything you have created. In Jesus's name. Amen."

Day 1  (GOOD)

When your mom and dad say that something "is good for you," what do they usually mean? Aren't they saying that something will make you better, stronger, safer, or more alive? It's something that'll cause you to flourish and thrive.

Did you know that God talks like this too? Read Psalm 92:1.

> It is good to give thanks to the LORD, to sing praises to your name, O Most High. Psalm 92:1

▶ Think about this verse and write it down in your own words.

Read Psalm 147:1.

> Praise the LORD! For it is good to sing praises to our God; for it is pleasant, and a song of praise is fitting. Psalm 147:1

▶ Put these two verses together. What do Psalm 92:1 and Psalm 147:1 say about worship? How do they describe it?

When you worship God, it's *good for you*! You were created to find "the good life"—the one that's full of treasuring and delighting in God with all your heart (Psalm 37:4; Mark 12:30).

Day 2 (BAD)

In the garden of Eden, Eve and Adam should have loved and treasured God more than anything else. However . . . read Genesis 3:6.

> So when the woman saw that the tree was good for food, and that it was a delight to the eyes, and that the tree was to be desired to make one wise, she took of its fruit and ate, and she also gave some to her husband who was with her, and he ate. Genesis 3:6

○ List all the benefits that disobeying God seemed to offer Eve.

○ At the moment of her temptation, what was Eve treasuring most?

○ Think about something you did recently that was wrong. Why did you do it? What did you really want in your heart? Often the thing we want (treasure, worship) is one—or more—of the following:

❏ control   ❏ power
❏ comfort   ❏ pleasure
❏ acceptance   ❏ fame
❏ stuff

○ Were these benefits wrong in themselves? What made them sinful for Eve to pursue? (Hint: read Genesis 2:16–17.)

○ Which of these do you find yourself wanting most regularly? Pray about understanding how these things can lead you toward sin. How can you treasure the Lord more than these things?

Day 3 (NEW)

In the Old Testament, their "worship services" happened as people brought their sacrifices to the tabernacle or temple. Today you probably go to church on Sunday. But the New Testament says something amazing about worship. Read Romans 12:1.

> I appeal to you therefore, brothers, by the mercies of God, to present your bodies as a living sacrifice, holy and acceptable to God, which is your spiritual worship. Romans 12:1

◗ According to this verse, what is the "sacrifice" that God wants from you in worship today?

THINK ABOUT IT

Do you realize what the Bible is saying? God doesn't need your singing or your Bible time. In fact, he doesn't need worship from you. He wants *you*—all of you! That's how you worship God—by giving your whole life, every day of the week.

◗ Re-read Romans 12:1 (above). Take a moment to write out a prayer thanking the Lord for his mercy (his love, forgiveness, and help). Because he has given everything for you, express how you want to give everything for him.

Say "ahh"

Ahhhhhh! If you have ever drunk a cold soft drink on a hot day, you know this sound.

But did you know that the soda company Coca-Cola owns the internet domain name featuring the words "ahh," "ahhh," and "ahhhhh"? In fact, it actually owns all the domain names for "ahh," from two *h*'s up to 61 *h*'s.

Almost every commercial or ad that shows people drinking soda also includes those people breathing out a refreshing "ahhh"! They can't help it! It's the natural reaction to something so cool and delicious.

The "ahh" is a response the same way that worship is a response. As we come to realize who God is and what he's like (by reading his Word), we respond—not with "ahh," but in thankfulness, delight, reliance, and obedience. So if you want to improve your worship experiences, don't focus on your worship.

Instead focus on God in his Word. Ask God to give you clearer glimpses of himself. The more you see his breathtaking mercy, his authentic compassion, his limitless ability, and his brilliant insight, the more your heart will respond accordingly. That's worship.[6]

WEEK EIGHT
RELATING TO PARENTS

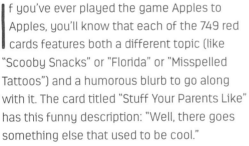

If you've ever played the game Apples to Apples, you'll know that each of the 749 red cards features both a different topic (like "Scooby Snacks" or "Florida" or "Misspelled Tattoos") and a humorous blurb to go along with it. The card titled "Stuff Your Parents Like" has this funny description: "Well, there goes something else that used to be cool."

It's hard being a kid, living with mom and dad. How uncool, right? Wouldn't it be great if you could just change one thing (or twenty!) about them? Usually friends aren't nearly as difficult to get along with. But the reality is that the deepest relationships are usually the most difficult—because you really get an up-close view of that person's strengths, limitations, and flaws. So if you can't *change* mom and dad, how do you handle your parents? The best place to start is to talk to God about it.

PRAYER

"Father, you are a good father, all the time. I really don't get my mom and dad sometimes, but you do. You made them. Please help me grow in my understanding of my parents, as well as in my love for them. Help me see them the way you see them. In Jesus's name. Amen."

Day 1  (GOOD)

Today we're going to look at God's original and **good** design for parents. Read Matthew 7:11.

> [Jesus said,] "If you then, who are evil, know how to give good gifts to your children, how much more will your Father who is in heaven give good things to those who ask him!" Matthew 7:11

● According to Jesus's teaching in this verse, what does any parent like to do for their children?

This means that despite the Fall, as a general rule sinful parents are still good parents. Remember the goalpost story from week three? Most moms and dads have not "bent" their role as parents beyond recognition.

● What is one area of goodness in your parents that you can thank the Lord for today? (Be sure to thank your mom or dad too.)

Day 2 (BAD)

The Bible agrees with you that parents don't have it all figured out. Sometimes they won't let you do what you want. And they can give what seem to be awfully weak reasons for saying no. (*arrghh!*) But God never promises that parents will be perfect. Instead, he's very realistic about it. God knows that your mom and dad are doing the best they can. Read Hebrews 12:9–10.

> [9] Besides this, we have had earthly fathers who disciplined us and we respected them. Shall we not much more be subject to the Father of spirits and live? [10] For they disciplined us for a short time as it seemed best to them, but he disciplines us for our good, that we may share his holiness. Hebrews 12:9–10

▶ What phrase in Hebrews 12:9–10 says that parents aren't perfect?

Now read Ephesians 6:1–3.

> [1] Children, obey your parents in the Lord, for this is right. [2] "Honor your father and mother" (this is the first commandment with a promise), [3] "that it may go well with you and that you may live long in the land." Ephesians 6:1–3

▶ List all the ways, given in this passage, that you should treat your parents, regardless of their imperfections.

Pause and ask the Lord to help you keep treating your parents as he wants you to.

Day 3 (NEW)

Today we look at how Jesus makes your relationship with your parents "**new.**"
Read Luke 14:26.

> [Jesus said,] "If anyone comes to me and does not hate his own father and mother and wife and children and brothers and sisters, yes, and even his own life, he cannot be my disciple." Luke 14:26

▶ What surprising thing does Jesus require from anyone who wants to be his follower ("my disciple")?

▶ How can Jesus command you to "hate" your parents? Read Matthew 10:37 (below) to explore what this "hating" looks like. Explain it in your own words.

> [Jesus said,] "Whoever loves father or mother more than me is not worthy of me, and whoever loves son or daughter more than me is not worthy of me." Matthew 10:37

God wants you to treat your parents with love and respect (Mark 7:10–13). But Jesus is teaching that you must love God *more* than you love your parents. Your love for your parents could seem like "hate" in comparison with your love for Jesus.

▶ Can you imagine ways you might make your family or parents a higher priority than God? (Hint: Think about things you enjoy about your family and parents. Where might these be bent and become too important?) Write down your thoughts.

HONOR YOUR PARENTS

Michael Oh had a choice to make. After becoming a Christian and going to college, he started to realize that the Lord was leading him to become a missionary. He also knew his parents wouldn't like it. Here's Michael's story in his own words.

I was a senior at the University of Pennsylvania, and after church I would often go to lunch with my parents. One Sunday, we went to a Chinese restaurant right near the campus, and I told my father that I wanted to be a missionary. And he said to me, "No." I said, "Dad, I appreciate everything you have done for me and for my sister, Tina." (My parents came to this country with three hundred dollars in their pockets, and lived in a tiny apartment over a Laundromat. And my father worked 120-hour weeks. And so I was trying to explain to my dad—this man whom I spent most of my life trying to please, to earn his love and affection—how my faith which had become so important to me had now moved me to the decision to want to be a missionary.)

So I said, "Dad, thank you for all that you've done for me and my sister. We are who we are, and we are where we are because of the sacrifices you and mom have made, but I refuse to live my life just trying to work hard so I can get into a good college and get a good job and make lots of money so that one day my kids will have every opportunity to get into a good college and get a good job so their kids can have every opportunity to get into college and get a good job and make lots of money, until Jesus returns. I refuse to live my life like that."

That was the start for me of how to understand "honor your father and mother." Your parents may say, "Choose: us or Jesus." And at that moment with fear and trembling and tears in your eyes, I pray that you will have the boldness to say, "I choose Jesus." For many that may bring the price of being disowned or even losing their very life. But Jesus makes it clear, if there is a choice, choose him."[7]

In 2004, Michael moved to Japan, where he founded a school for training pastors, a cafe, and a church-planting ministry. Since 2013, Michael has also been the leader of the Lausanne Movement, a worldwide missions organization.

WEEK NINE
RELATING TO FRIENDS

Texting can be awesome . . . and annoying. Tech-challenged family members might send "lots of love" (LOL), and some friends just can't take a hint!

> Hi!!!!!!!!
>
> Whatsup?????
>
> How was your night?
>
> ?????
>
> Whatcha doing today?
>
> Headed to a friends!

But, on the positive side, your phone can be an easy way to keep in touch with friends. Obviously friendships have been around a lot longer than texting or the latest app. This week we're going to look at what the Bible says about friendship.

PRAYER

"Father, thanks for the friends you've given to me. Help me be a good friend to those who need friends. Most of all let me learn to enjoy Jesus's friendship more. In his name. Amen."

Day 1 (GOOD)

▶ If you took special time to spend just with God—reading his Word and talking to him—where would you go? What would you do? Stop and try to imagine the most spiritual and godly scenario you can dream up.

It's hard to think of anything better than what God created for Adam in the garden of Eden. Here's what Adam enjoyed: no distractions or difficulties, only the most stunning surroundings, good food, fun stuff to do, and the closest relationship with God. It was all very good, which makes what God said next so incredibly surprising. Read Genesis 2:18a.

> Then the LORD God said, "It is not good that the man should be alone." Genesis 2:18a

Without *other people*, even the best life—and the best Christian life—would be incomplete. God designed you to enjoy friendship.

▶ How can friendship help you? Read Ecclesiastes 4:9-10 and Proverbs 27:17 and write down an answer. Add other ideas that come to mind.

> Two are better than one, because they have a good reward for their toil. For if they fall, one will lift up his fellow. But woe to him who is alone when he falls and has not another to lift him up! Ecclesiastes 4:9-10
>
> Iron sharpens iron, and one man sharpens another. Proverbs 27:17

▶ Take 45 seconds and thank the Lord for providing friends (or ask him to provide friends).

Day 2 (BAD)

God gave you friends. After all, the whole concept of friendship was his idea! Friends help each other, enjoy each other, and encourage each other. But, as you know, friends can be difficult too.

▶ Describe some characteristics of a not-so-good friend. What do you think a bad friend is like?

▶ Read Proverbs 16:28 and Psalm 38:11 (below). What are some things that make for a bad friend according to these verses?

A contrary person spreads conflict, and a gossip separates close friends. Proverbs 16:28 CSB

My loved ones and friends stand back from my affliction, and my relatives stand at a distance. Psalm 38:11 CSB

▶ How do you think your friends would describe you?

▶ Give two specific and recent examples of how you have not been a good friend.

▶ Take some time to talk to the Lord about how you could be a better friend. Is there anything you need to ask him or others to forgive you for?

Day 3 (NEW)

Friends are part of God's good design for life in this world. They help you and encourage you. The wrong kind of friends may influence you in bad directions. But Jesus came not just to give you good friends but to help make you into a good friend. How? Let's dive in.

▶ Read John 15:12–13. What do these verses show you about what Jesus's death has done to transform your relationship with him? How does he set the best example for friendship?

{ [Jesus said,] "This is my commandment, that you love one another as I have loved you. Greater love has no one than this, that someone lay down his life for his friends." John 15:12–13

Jesus didn't die to make good people, attractive people, or nice people into his friends. He came to die for sinners—men and women who were born with the desire to go their own way, instead of God's way (Romans 5:6, 10).

▶ If you belong to Jesus, if he has brought you into friendship with God, what's your plan to be the kind of friend Jesus has been to you? How will you be the kind of friend who befriends even those who are needy, who don't have much in common with you, who can't pay you back? (Jesus talks about this in Luke 14:12–14.)

aLL iN THE SaME BOaT

In his book, *The Boys in the Boat*, Daniel James Brown tells the all-but-forgotten adventure of nine young men in their unlikely quest to win the gold medal in rowing for the United States at the 1936 Berlin Olympics. Leading up to this Olympic pursuit, the story follows the life of Joe Rantz, who rose from a difficult past and dysfunctional family to find in his teammates a brotherhood of friends.

It didn't take Joe long to discover that rowing was not a solo sport. Rowing wasn't about him. He had to focus on others. Victory required eight individuals to each fill his own

unique role yet in perfect harmony and coordination with the team. Together these eight young men learned to work together. They sacrificed their own comforts, their own styles, their own desires—for the good of others. They were friends, and they were teammates.

And that's what made them so unbeatable!

> **[When] all were merged into one smoothly working machine; they were, in fact, a poem of motion, a symphony of swinging blades. . . . If one fellow in an orchestra was playing out of tune, or playing at a different tempo, the whole piece would naturally be ruined.** [8]

True friends serve others. With the Lord's help and example, they don't focus on themselves, and they don't focus on the weaknesses of others. They sacrifice themselves for the success of others.

WEEK TEN
RELATING TO FAMILY

I am the older brother to three younger sisters. Before the youngest was born, I had hoped for a brother, but alas, I got another sister. (On the other extreme, my wife grew up with two brothers and no sister.) And during my growing-up years, I have to admit there were times that we fought and argued. But mostly we just got on each other's nerves.

When we were younger, I would tease them and call them names that annoyed them. Then I would hide their toys just to watch them get frustrated. ("Brother" is, after all, only one letter away from "bother.")

Of course, when I would get in trouble, they would laugh at me—where I could see them but our parents could not. It seemed that Ephesians 4:32 was our mother's favorite verse ("Be kind to one another . . . ").

But over time something strange happened. We actually began to enjoy each other. Seem impossible with someone in *your* family? How does this kind of thing happen? That's something we'll explore this week. But first, let's pray about it.

PRAYER

"Father, you made everything according to your good design. And those plans include members of my family. Please help me see more clearly just how good you designed my family. In Jesus's name. Amen."

Day 1 (GOOD)

▶ You're going to like this verse. Read Proverbs 17:17 (below) and write it down word-for-word, but substitute some names of your family members in place of the word "brother."

{ A friend loves at all times, and a brother is born for adversity. Proverbs 17:17

After writing this verse you might say, "Yup, he or she was born for *adversity*." And it may seem like your brother, sister, or other family member was put on planet Earth just to make your life difficult. But this verse actually says the opposite of what you may have thought.

This verse teaches that when life gets difficult, your family members are there to help. God gave family to you as a gift. They help you in tough times, in "adversity."

◉ Can you think of a time (any time) that someone in your family helped you when you were having a hard time? Describe in detail what you remember.

◉ What can you do to be that kind of help to others today (perhaps a family member or a friend)? Pray about it and write down some ideas.

Day 2 (BAD)

Read Genesis 4:2–8 (below). This is the story of the first family, the first set of brothers. Yet its truths fit any relationship.

> 2 And again, she bore his brother Abel. Now Abel was a keeper of sheep, and Cain a worker of the ground. 3 In the course of time Cain brought to the Lord an offering of the fruit of the ground, 4 and Abel also brought of the firstborn of his flock and of their fat portions. And the Lord had regard for Abel and his offering, 5 but for Cain and his offering he had no regard. So Cain was very angry, and his face fell. 6 The Lord said to Cain, "Why are you angry, and why has your face fallen? 7 If you do well, will you not be accepted? And if you do not do well, sin is crouching at the door. Its desire is contrary to you, but you must rule over it." 8 Cain spoke to Abel his brother. And when they were in the field, Cain rose up against his brother Abel and killed him. Genesis 4:2–8

▶ Why do you think Cain became angry with Abel? It may help to go back and re-read the story.

Devotional

● Now read James 4:2 (below). Circle the word *want* in this verse.

> You want what you don't have, so you scheme and kill to
> get it. You are jealous of what others have, but you can't
> get it, so you fight and wage war to take it away from
> them. Yet you don't have what you want because you
> don't ask God for it. James 4:2 NLT

● In your own words, what reason does this verse give for why fights take place?

● Based on today's verses, think about your relationship with family members (or even close friends). What kinds of things do you fight or argue about? What "want" or desire might be at the heart of your conflict? Take a minute to talk to the Lord about this "want."

Day 3 (NEW)

▶ Read Luke 8:19–21 (below). In these verses, who is trying to get to Jesus while he is teaching the Word of God to those crowded around him?

> ¹⁹ Then his mother and his brothers came to him, but they could not reach him because of the crowd. ²⁰ And he was told, "Your mother and your brothers are standing outside, desiring to see you." ²¹ But he answered them, "My mother and my brothers are those who hear the word of God and do it." Luke 8:19–21

▶ Read these verses again. What did someone say to Jesus that was intended to encourage him to wrap things up and talk to his family?

▶ What surprising thing does Jesus say back?

▶ Even if you have terrible family members or no family at all, if you are a Christian you are part of God's family. Thank the Lord for making you part of his own family. Then write down one way you can encourage one of your brothers or sisters in Christ, this week.

IN CLOSING

BROTHERLY LOVE?

Check all that apply.

☐ You are regularly annoyed by an individual in your family.
☐ You have pulled an awesome prank on a member of your family.
☐ You have thought about trying to sell a family member at a garage sale.

If you've checked any of these boxes, keep reading. The reality is that it's hard to get along with people you're around all the time. You know everything about them—and every bit of it drives you crazy. That's just how family can be sometimes.

But did you know that it's pretty common for family members to actually become good friends, especially as they get older? Hopefully, you already consider your brothers or sisters or other family members as friends. But the older you get, the better friends they can become.

Did you also know that during your whole lifetime, some of the people who have known you the longest will probably be those in your family? When you're seventy (hard to imagine, I know!), you will have known your siblings or cousins, for example, for almost that entire time. And almost no one else will have known you that long.

Here are some good relationship guidelines for getting along with people in your family. (These guidelines apply to friends too.)

1. Always treat the other person with respect and thoughtfulness. (They are created in God's image, remember?)

2. If something doesn't belong to you, you usually have no reason to touch it. (Don't mess with other people's stuff without their permission.)

3. If you're trying just to have a little fun, and it's not fun for the other person, then don't do it.

4. Don't have fun or make a joke at the expense of another person.

5. Wherever possible, take the initiative to move toward people and problems in love and wisdom.

6. Privileges (like owning stuff, being older, stronger, smarter, etc.) bring greater opportunities to serve other people (including people in your family).

WEEK ELEVEN
DIFFICULT RELATIONSHIPS

Every person is different . . . Some are just more different than others.

At least it seems that way. Being around some people may make you want to scream! So what grates on you the most? The sloppy, messy slob? The smacking, noisy eater? The loud laughing jokester? The social media goofball? The emotional drama king or queen?

Don't we all find different things (and people) annoying? Wouldn't it be great if everyone were more normal? More like us?

Does the Bible even talk about difficult people? Let's find out.

PRAYER

"Father, would you help me learn how to relate to people that I find difficult to be around? Would you give me love and patience with them— just as you treat me with love and patience? In Jesus's name. Amen."

Day 1  (GOOD)

● Read Psalm 139:14–16. According to verse 14, what words describe how God has made each person (even people whom you may think of as "difficult")?

> ¹⁴ I will praise you because I have been remarkably and wondrously made. Your works are wondrous, and I know this very well. ¹⁵ My bones were not hidden from you when I was made in secret, when I was formed in the depths of the earth. ¹⁶ Your eyes saw me when I was formless; all my days were written in your book and planned before a single one of them began. Psalm 139:14–16 CSB

● Re-read verse 16. How much of your life, and everyone else's life (even people very different than you), has been carefully designed by God?

THINK ABOUT IT

God made each human as a unique individual. There are no identical thumbprints; there are no identical people. Each person has his or her special mix of talents, personality, experiences, and family characteristics. You might find someone especially annoying who is very *different* than you, or who is actually quite *similar* to you in some way.

So, when you're around that difficult person, of course the things you find obnoxious come through loud and clear. But you're probably missing what's not so obvious to you. What are that person's *strengths*? Their *good* qualities? Remember, God has made each person in his image (Genesis 1:27), and he's also given them wonderful qualities you may not have recognized yet.

▶ So stop and think about a difficult person in your life. Now, without mentioning his or her name, what good qualities does this person have? What are his or her strengths?

Day 2 (BAD)

Read Mark 10:13–16.

¹³ And they were bringing children to him that he might touch them, and the disciples rebuked them. ¹⁴ But when Jesus saw it, he was indignant and said to them, "Let the children come to me; do not hinder them, for to such belongs the kingdom of God. ¹⁵ Truly, I say to you, whoever does not receive the kingdom of God like a child shall not enter it." ¹⁶ And he took them in his arms and blessed them, laying his hands on them. Mark 10:13–16

▶ Why do you think the disciples didn't want parents to bring their children to Jesus? (Hint: Think about little kids and think about the busy schedule of Jesus's ministry.)

▶ Here's the point: If there's light, there's shadow. Where there's strength, there's weakness. How did Jesus respond—and how should you respond—to the weakness and limitations in the story above?

Pray about how you can treat others (with their weaknesses and limitations) today.

Day 3 (NEW)

Jesus gives us (1) the example to imitate and (2) the strength to deal with difficult people. Read John 13:3–9, 12 (below). Underline the parts of the story (words/actions) that might have annoyed you if you had been there.

> 3 Jesus . . . laid aside his outer garments, and taking a towel, tied it around his waist. 5 Then he poured water into a basin and began to wash the disciples' feet and to wipe them with the towel that was wrapped around him. 6 He came to Simon Peter, who said to him, "Lord, do you wash my feet?" 7 Jesus answered him, "What I am doing you do not understand now, but afterward you will understand." 8 Peter said to him, "You shall never wash my feet." Jesus answered him, "If I do not wash you, you have no share with me." 9 Simon Peter said to him, "Lord, not my feet only but also my hands and my head!" . . . 12 When he had washed their feet and put on his outer garments and resumed his place, he said to them, "Do you understand what I have done to you?"   John 13:3–9, 12

● How does Jesus respond to Peter (in word and in action)?

● List five ways you can try to help others today (even difficult people).

● If you are a Christian, list five ways that Jesus has served and helped you.

JESUS RECOGNIZES THE TOUCH OF FAITH

During Jesus's ministry, there was a time that he and his disciples were trying to squeeze their way through a packed crowd of people (Mark 5:24–31). It was elbow-to-elbow crowding, pushing, and inching along. And in the middle of all that, a woman who needed healing reached out and touched Jesus's coat.

And she was instantly healed! Jesus knew what had happened, and he wanted to talk to the healed woman. So he asked, "Who touched me?" The disciples had no clue about any of this. They said something like, "Everyone's pushing and shoving, and you ask, 'Who touched me?'"

You can almost see Jesus smiling at his disciples' comment as he turned to speak with the healed woman. Even in a situation that many might find annoying, Jesus found an opportunity to serve.

WEEK TWELVE
BROKEN RELATIONSHIPS

When I was in college, my car was a ten-year-old Toyota Corolla. It had been white when it was new. Yet not even the passing of years could change that it was just a compact station wagon. Ugly car . . . but I loved it!

It didn't matter that it had been my *dad's* car, because now it was *my* car. I could drive where and when I wanted. I could go out to eat with my friends and go home on the weekends. But there were also problems.

After awhile, the car didn't start when I turned the key. I tried to get it fixed, but that didn't last. So I could never tell when it would start and when it wouldn't. My friends and I would pray and try to start it. When it didn't start, we'd give it a push in order to jump-start it. Eventually, we began calling it the "prayer mobile." It was great to have a car, but a lot of trouble too.

But car troubles don't compare to *people troubles*. There's a good chance that most of the drama in your life is related to people, not stuff. Parents, friends, teachers, relatives—these characters in life bring the highest joys and deepest pain.

Why are so many problems today related to people? It's not new. Conflicts and issues between people have been around since the beginning of human history. What do you do about it? That's what we're going to look at this week.

PRAYER

"Lord, help me think more clearly about the people in my life, especially in those relationships that seem broken. Help me act more kindly too. For Jesus's sake. Amen."

Day 1 (GOOD)

▶ Read Genesis 2:20 (below). In this verse, underline the words that describe Adam's wife.

> He [Adam] gave names to all the livestock, all the birds of the sky, and all the wild animals. But still there was no helper just right for him. Genesis 2:20 NLT

God prepared Adam for Eve by having him name all the animals. After identifying each kind, Adam knew that none of these creatures was "just right" for him. However, Eve was another story. As another human, Eve was like Adam. Yet she was different from him—he was man and she was woman. Alike, yet not alike (Genesis 2:21-23).

Even before sin came into the world, God designed people to get along with others who were like, but not exactly like, them. Differences in people are his idea.

▶ Are your friends all the same as you are? Do you have trouble having relationships with people who are different from you? Write out a prayer asking God to help you see others as God sees them. Ask God to help you appreciate differences in the people he created.

Day 2 (BAD)

Read Genesis 3:12–13. In this passage, look for the effect that sin had on Adam and Eve's relationship.

> The man said, "The woman whom you gave to be with me, she gave me fruit of the tree, and I ate." Then the LORD God said to the woman, "What is this that you have done?" The woman said, "The serpent deceived me, and I ate."
> Genesis 3:12–13

○ Adam and Eve had both sinned and, feeling guilty, hid from God. What did Adam say when the Lord confronted him with his sin? Did he protect and support Eve?

○ Sin was pushing Adam and Eve apart. Now think about yourself and people you know. How does sin push you away from people who are different from you?

○ How would you describe Adam's words? (circle one)

loving

lying

blaming

helping

comforting

○ How do you think about kids in different economic circumstances from you? If they have more than you do, does envy cloud your thinking about who they really are and what they might be struggling with? Or, if they have less than you do, does pride tempt you to feel better than them?

Day 3 (NEW)

▶ Read Ephesians 2:14, 16 (below). What reason do these verses give for Jesus's death on the cross?

{ For he [Jesus] is our peace, who made both groups one and tore down the dividing wall of hostility . . . He did this so that he might reconcile both to God in one body through the cross by which he put the hostility to death. Ephesians 2:14, 16 CSB

DID YOU KNOW?

Jesus has united all people who follow him—even people from different countries, cultures, and groups—into one group. This means that as a Christian, you have more in common with other Christians who are super different from you than you have with your closest friend who is not a Christian.

◉ Think of someone you know who is a Christian but who is also quite different from you. List some things you have in common because you are both Christians.

◉ If your relationship with this person is broken, what next steps should you take to try to restore that relationship? (This can be difficult to handle. You may want to discuss it with a parent, teacher, or pastor.)

Keeping Your Balance

In 2007, Sam Wakeling did something no one had ever done before. He pedaled 105.57 miles across the country of Wales without his feet ever touching the ground. That's a long distance, but people ride that far all the time. What made Sam's ride unique—a world's record actually—was that he covered those miles riding a unicycle! Not a bicycle with two wheels—a unicycle, with only *one wheel*.

Now that's an accomplishment. Keeping your balance for that long is no simple feat. Unicycle riders are constantly trying to keep from falling forward and backward, not just balancing from side to side as on a regular bike.

The same balance is needed in challenging relationships. When someone else is being difficult, you can be tempted to *be angry*. At other times you want to *run away*. The first option goes on the offensive, and the second goes into hiding.

In most cases, God wants us to stay engaged and stay calm—to be lovingly truthful and helpful. It takes balance to keep from sliding off into either attack mode or escape mode. Christian author Ken Sande says that in conflict there are three kinds of people: peace-breakers, peace-fakers, and peace-makers.[9]

KEEPING BALANCE IN CHALLENGING RELATIONSHIPS

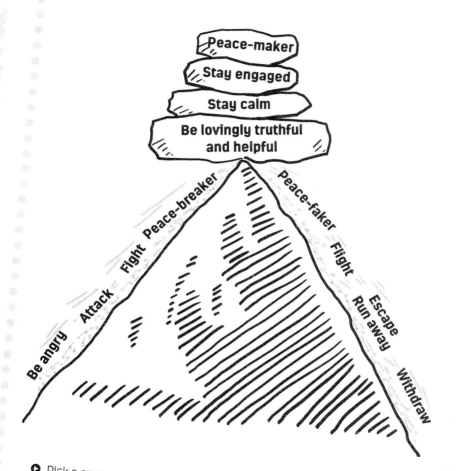

● Pick a spot on the slope. Where would you locate your own typical response to difficult people?

WEEK THIRTEEN
CHURCH RELATIONSHIPS

As we wrap up our study of relationships, let's talk about people at church. Why do you go to church? Is church a building for weekend meetings? Is it like doing your devotions with other people? Is it a time to meet with friends and struggle to understand what's being taught? Is it, as some say, a club for hypocrites?

What does the Bible say about church? The New Testament uses word pictures to illustrate what the church is. The church is like a "body" (1 Corinthians 12:27), like a "temple" (Ephesians 2:19–22), and like a "flock" of sheep (1 Peter 5:1–3). Each of these terms is collective (which means a collection of parts all put together, like grapes in a bunch or players on a team).

The church is a group of Christians who have committed to regularly meet together to give and receive encouragement. This happens as they talk, listen, and help each other; as they hear God's Word taught and read; and as they work together to trust and obey God.

But is all this really necessary? What if your devotions are more helpful than church teaching? Can't you do all that church stuff on your own or with your family? Let's explore why God invented the church.

PRAYER

"Father, thank you for giving your own Son for the church. Please help me grow in understanding why the church is important. In Jesus's name. Amen."

Day 1 (GOOD)

▶ Read Genesis 1:28 (below). According to this verse, what word best describes how many people God wanted on planet earth?

❏ one   ❏ several   ❏ some   ❏ a lot

{ And God blessed them. And God said to them, "Be fruitful and multiply and fill the earth and subdue it, and have dominion over the fish of the sea and over the birds of the heavens and over every living thing that moves on the earth." Genesis 1:28

The Old Testament reminds us of God's original design for the human race. He never intended for people to live by themselves (Genesis 2:18a). He made us to need others; and he put together a group—a large group—of people. After all, he called his followers "my people"—there were *many* individuals united together.

God made us for himself, and he made us for relationships with other people. And in the New Testament, God created the church—the gathering together of his people.

▶ List the names of five people (your age or adults) who you know and who know you at church.

▶ What are three ways that other people at church can help or encourage you in your relationship with Jesus?

Day 2 (BAD)

The church is good. It's part of God's plan. But today we're going to look at the "bad news" about church. Read the following verses from 1 Corinthians. Then circle the words that describe the sin that was taking place in this church.

> For it has been reported to me by Chloe's people that there is quarreling among you, my brothers.
> 1 Corinthians 1:11

> It is actually reported that there is sexual immorality among you, and of a kind that is not tolerated even among pagans. 1 Corinthians 5:1a

> Therefore, my beloved, flee from idolatry.
> 1 Corinthians 10:14

● What strikes you about all this sin in this church? As you read these verses, what stood out to you?

● How, according to these verses, did Paul (the author of 1 Corinthians) respond to all this sin in the church? Did he think their sin and mess was no big deal?

▶ Why do you think he wrote a letter to this messed up church?

THINK ABOUT IT

Don't be surprised when people at church let you down, when people sin and make awful mistakes. The church, after all, is filled with sinners. When you think about it—there's no other option. We're *all* sinners. And that means the church is not a perfect place. You will be disappointed and hurt— and you may even disappoint and hurt others. But that's usually not a good reason to give up on the church. Paul didn't. God didn't. Take a moment to pray for some people in your church that may have disappointed you. Pray and ask God to help you acknowledge times when you may have disappointed others.

Day 3 (NEW)

● How does Jesus make "bad" church stuff "new"? Read 1 Corinthians 1:2–7 (below). Remember the verses from Day 2 of this week? For today, underline all the *positive* things that Paul could honestly say about the same church, the one located in Corinth.

² To the church of God that is in Corinth, to those sanctified in Christ Jesus, called to be saints together with all those who in every place call upon the name of our Lord Jesus Christ, both their Lord and ours: ³ Grace to you and peace from God our Father and the Lord Jesus Christ. ⁴ I give thanks to my God always for you because of the grace of God that was given you in Christ Jesus, ⁵ that in every way you were enriched in him in all speech and all knowledge— ⁶ even as the testimony about Christ was confirmed among you— ⁷ so that you are not lacking in any spiritual gift, as you wait for the revealing of our Lord Jesus Christ. 1 Corinthians 1:2–7

● So, according to these verses, how should you treat other Christians who don't seem to get it? How do you respond to people who seem weak or immature in their faith?

● What about *your* spiritual maturity? Are you working with Jesus to become more like him? Are you discouraged that it is so hard or is taking so long? As you pray about it, ask the Lord to help you take the next step toward godly change. What is that next step? Who at church can you share this with?

TO EAT OR NOT TO EAT?

When I was in high school, sometimes church terrified me. When our church celebrated the Lord's Supper (otherwise known as the Lord's Table or Communion), our pastor would warn everyone not to eat the Lord's Supper "in an unworthy manner." He would read from 1 Corinthians 11 where Paul said that some people who had eaten "in an unworthy manner" had become sick or even died! So we were told to confess **all** our sins before participating in Communion. But what if we forgot a sin? Or what if we hadn't really confessed enough?

Then one day, years later, I realized what Paul meant about eating at the Lord's Table "in an unworthy manner." When the church in Corinth celebrated the Lord's Supper, they didn't just eat a small bit of bread and juice. The Lord's Supper was part of a church feast—a banquet. But there was a problem. Some rich people who didn't have to work would arrive early and start eating. A few hours later, when others

arrived, there wasn't much food left. Just scraps. The good stuff was gone.

Some people were acting important and not thinking about other members of the church. They were not "discerning the body" (1 Corinthians 11:29). They didn't realize that there were other people who were as important in Jesus's eyes. They were *all* members of Christ's body—he died for all of them and loved all of them equally!

The Lord's Supper was a time to gather around the table as a group, a church, and a family. But the church in Corinth was celebrating this get-together feast in "an unworthy manner." This was sin.

So when your church celebrates the Lord's Supper, if your parents allow you to participate, please take time to confess your sins to the Lord. That's always right to do. But remember that the Lord is calling you to his *table*. He's inviting you to sit together as a family, *his* family. So rely on his sacrifice on the cross to cover all your sins. And then eat and enjoy being together with Christ and his body!

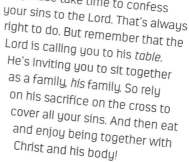
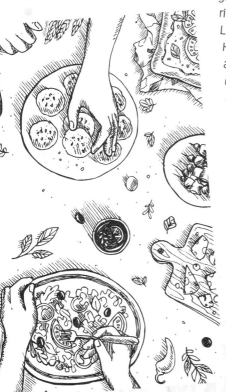

iStock.com/Adehoidar

Acknowledgments

I thank the Lord for the opportunity to have written this study. The perspective emphasized in *Radically Different*—using "good, bad, and new" as lenses through which to view the world—has changed *my* life. It's helped me better understand the Lord and how to live more wisely in the world he has made. I first learned about this approach in 2007, through an online sermon series by Pastor Bernard Bell, who has graciously given permission to use his good, bad, and new categories for this study.

Additionally, this study wouldn't exist without the efforts of many people. Several have been extremely helpful discussion partners through the writing process: Dr. Bruce Ashford, Dr. Roger Erdvig, Dr. Blake Hardcastle, Dr. Curtis Hill, Rev. Chris Morris, and Dr. Bryan Smith. I'm grateful for the support and encouragement of New Growth Press: the leadership of Karen Teears, the guidance of Barbara Juliani, and the insights of Nancy Winter and the rest of the editorial team. I'm also thrilled to once again team up with illustrator Scot McDonald, whose design makes written words so much more fun to read.

Finally, a word of appreciation for my son, Micah, to whom this book is dedicated. He gave up part of his summer break to read Dad's book and provided great feedback. I pray this book encourages him and every reader toward the Lord and all his ways.

Notes

1. Michael Williams, in Dane Ortlund, "What's the Message of the Bible in One Sentence," Strawberry-Rhubarb Thelogy, January 12, 2011, http://dogmadoxa.blogspot.com/2011/01/whats-message-of-bible-in-one-sentence.html.

2. C. S. Lewis, *Mere Christianity* (New York: HarperOne, 1952), 175–76.

3. Adapted from George Herbert, "The Elixir" in George Herbert, *The Complete English Works*, ed. Ann Pasternak Slater, in Everyman's Library (New York: Alfred A. Knopf, 1995), 180.

4. The concepts of "structure" and "direction" are taken from Albert M. Wolters, *Creation Regained: Biblical Basics for a Reformational Worldview*, 2nd ed. (Grand Rapids: Eerdmans, 2005), 87–89.

5. Adapted from Bruce Ashford and Chris Pappalardo, *One Nation Under God: A Christian Hope for American Politics* (Nashville: B & H Publishing Group, 2015), 16.

6. Adapted from John Piper, "The Worship of the Christian Leader," November 8, 1991, transcript and audio, https://www.desiringgod.org/messages/the-worship-of-the-christian-leader.

7. Adapted from Michael Oh, "Honor Thy Father and Mother," lecture, CROSS Conference, December 29, 2013, audio, http://crossforthenations.org/media/2014/01/honor-thy-father-and-mother/. Used by permission.

8. Daniel James Brown, *The Boys in the Boat: Nine Americans and Their Epic Quest for Gold at the 1936 Berlin Olympics* (New York: Viking, 2013), 234–35, 249.

9. Adapted from Ken Sande, "Staying on Top of Conflict," Relational Wisdom 360, accessed August 2018, https://rw360.org/slippery-slope/.